Down

Down

Here on This Earth

---

sparrow santo

Contents

Introduction .... *viii*

Prologue: The Land and the Sea .... *ix*

Of the Land

Across Earth-Land 2
Love-Pockets 3
Wildflower 4
Child-Flower 5
Forest in the Foggy Morning Silence 6
In Febr'ary 7
Trees of Winter 8
Tree of Spring 9
To Be or Not to Be 10
Be 11
Rains 12
Slowly 13
Deeper 14
Room to Grow 15
Maranta (Mantra) 16
Room to Go 17
Motion and Shift 18
Matters of Perspective (One Whole) 19
Matters of Perspective (One's Whole) 20
Someplace in Time 21
Time (Between) 22
Time (Forward and Behind) 23
Pinecones 24
Autumn Leaves 25
Caledonia 26
On Rainey Park Fields 27
Traces 28
Like a Lolling Stone 29
Peace 30

Of the Sea

The Ocean	32
Notes on the Sea	33
One Whole	34
Pas de deux	35
Making Waves	36
Movement	37
From You to Me	38
Explorers of a Boundless Deep	39
Submergence	40
To Source	42
I Go to the Water	43
At the Edges of Seas	44
Transform	45
Beauty in the Broken (Sea Glass)	46
Reflections	47
The Holy Sea	49
Washed Away	50
Trinity	51
Forge	52
The Up and the Sea	53
Momentum	54
Peace (Reprise)	55
Epilogue: Here on This Earth	56
Glossary	58
Elsewhere	66

I wander
I notice
I wonder

"Then God said, 'Let the waters under the heavens be gathered together into one place, and let the dry land appear'; and it was so. And God called the dry land Earth, and the gathering together of the waters He called Seas. And God saw that it was good." (Genesis 1:9-10 New King James Version)

For my presence here—as one witness to the wondrous workings of Your wide and wild world, Your *good* Earth—I am humbly grateful. ~ss

Introduction

The Earth—a brilliant work of art—is ripe in sensorial wonder and is inspiring to the creative human mind. It is a divine sanctuary—one sacred house built to shelter, nourish, and sustain all living forms birthed across its ever-circling expanse. It is a marvelous ecosystem of infinite tidbits—perfectly crafted, elaborately interwoven, and synchronously coexistent in design. The Earth—it is our place for now.

Something keeps us here; something pulls us **down** to remain grounded upon this plane. A force, surely. A power known, perhaps, by different names: Gravity…God…*Something*. Aye, something greater to gently remind us of our mere-ness.

If we are curious—if we are studious and receptive to each Greater truth reflected within the green, brown, and blueprints of this Earth's design—might we come to better understand all presence here upon it? Might we come to better understand this Earth as our downward and primordial domain?

Prologue: The Land and the Sea

Looking down from up
high above the Earth
there is not one person to be seen

for all who dwell upon the land
blend into the land
and all that Are
become
one part of the Earth

Looking down from up
high above the Earth
there is only the land and the sea

Of the Land

Across Earth-Land

As I travel across Earth-land, I see
many things

> things that grow
> things that cover the Earth's floor
> things that rise to fill the space above

Here on this Earth
there is all this
and no absence of Earth

There is one me
always
in my one small place
with a remainder of space
filled
by the absence of me

Here on this Earth
I am but a guest
given one invitation
for this
one Earth-day

May there be more

I pray
and I remove my hat
and I very humbly tread my feet

Love-Pockets

We walk upon an Earth that is abundant with Spirit: A treasure trove of trillions glistens deep inside the pockets of its rich and finely woven expanse. I think about this often—several times throughout each bustling New York day and any time I become distracted from myself by the glimpse of a perched lady beetle, for example, or the life that teems from a rippling sidewalk rain puddle. It reminds of that moment when all the white and swirling bits inside of a snow globe finally settle, leaving only a crystal-clear image and a silent, frozen interlude.

The time that divides my human world stands still.

I become reconnected with the simple essence of Being as my soul erupts in exclamation: *I am here . . . and you are all here too!*

I pause in the presence of these precious forms, and I pray that they will choose to remain in mine. I wonder about them—about the brilliance of such pure and heavenly science—and I wonder if they are wondering about me. With but a few beats and breaths, my heart bursts in the most bountiful bliss of blessing: *I feel Love!*

Love is what the Earth holds so dearly inside its pockets for all those who seek it. Have you felt it too?

Wildflower

Pure optic confection

> Earth's brilliant conception
> allures all attention
> t'ward the world of its Small

Child-Flower

Soft, layered perfection

    exquisite reflection
    of one deep in connection
    with Earth's curious Small

Forest in the Foggy Morning Silence

In the foggy morning silence, I come inclined to climb their incline
    one steep that seeks to keep me sliding back to meet defeat
Stoic witnesses to my naivety tower high far 'yond my reach
with nae a wince for any crunch of Fallen from beneath my fumbling feet

In Febr'ary

In Febr'ary

when the trees bear
branches' bare bones

every bird tenant is seen

I look for birds
every day up high
'thin the Rainey trees—aye, high
and I
see birds

and they notice me

And in Febr'ary
'midst the bare-boned trees
when the tiny sparrows' song-breaths
freeze
I do not feel alone
    not 'lone

I nae one day
feel 'lone

Trees of Winter

Limbs
stark down to bark bones
each long, frozen night

Still, they stand tall
Still, they reach t'ward the light

Tree of Spring

Each ring adorned is wisdom worn

    a promise sworn to have
    and to hold our forms within her strong
    and home-sweet-h-arbored hands

Sun to sun—each Earthen breath
seed and fruit, or shading bough…

Might it be a selfless love that allows a self to grow?

To Be or Not to Be

I am drawn to where the East River edges upon Astoria; Hell Gate it is called. A penetrable guardrail runs along the whirling waters, aiming to keep wayward wanderers within some limits. Perhaps it is only meant to serve as a passive warning—a suggestive Enter at Your Own Risk that has kept me overstepping every time.

I find many small trees and shrubs along the rocky and vertically sloping banks pushing outwards through abrasive stone piles and growing almost parallel to the waters below. They remain so deeply rooted in their source, defying the gravitational forces that work against them. Here they adapt and find a new way to grow. What can be, after all, their other option?

Aye, I am pulled to where the East River edges upon Astoria as a witness to one of nature's sacred parables. I have gained the wisdom to Be and embrace my odds or—simply—cease to Be.

Be

Because there is
balance
and because there are
opposites
there is always a choice of two

The most fundamental
is simple

    Choose to Be or not Be

The next progresses accordingly

    Remain as is
    or evolve

Rains

There are darker times

There are storms
and there are rains

There are drops that bring us growth

Slowly

A winter must end for a spring to begin
Cold, when it fades, it fades slowly
Warmth, when born then, will, too, be as slow
Aye, these things of the Earth I have come sure to know
learning slowly
    slowly through time

Snow cedes to rain; what grows, grows again
up from every small place that fills up larger land
We, too, shall progress and Become through process
very slowly
    slowly through time

Deeper

I have stood for great lengths very still
and with two feet bare 'pon the ground
stretching as wide as two small feet may go

> then wider
> and much wider still

My weight, a cascade in downward waves

> through jaw
> through chest
> through back
> through waist

One avalanche that plummets down
    down for two feet to bear

Gravity
    Earth's warm embrace
we greet as I press with both feet placed
down to this sacred garden space
as a stamp to hold claim o'er my land. We expand

this I know, but when soles root below
souls will grow
deeper

> and much deeper still

Room to Grow

At the center of a vast
field lush with tall grass
I sit small
to eye miles of expanse. Aye

here I seem mere
though one Great message clear

> *All who start small*
> *must keep room to Grow*

Maranta (Mantra)

If we root our selves here in the Earth

If we plant our soles firm
Keep well, and take care

If we close tight in prayer every evening
Then unfold to the light of each day

May we grow without span, without seasoning

Find a way to lose thought
For the green, it thinks naught

May we no longer know wrong or reasoning

Forget time, forget age, and keep nothing in claim
Save for souls set to pass on t'ward yonder domain

If we root our selves here in the Earth

Room to Go

At the center of a vast
Trossachs vale, golden grass
sways to each ripple
'thin the Ard's liquid 'spanse

One mallard swims 'lone
and a wise Earth makes known

> *All—great and small*
> *must keep room to Go*

Motion and Shift

Rotating to peruse self
Revolving to pursue light
Evolving as plates shift to bring change

Bound down to the grounds
of this thoroughfare

    a furrowed, fair, and aged
    mother's skin

we'll rise high 'pon her pillars
and sink low 'thin her glens

Bound down, we are motion and shift

Matters of Perspective (One Whole)

Are you digging a hole, or are you piling a mountain?
It is all a matter of perspective.

Upon Earth's canvas, we experience both positive and negative space. Together, the two create one whole, and there exists no absence of the other—only relocation and movement.

> Walk from your place, and you will fill a space elsewhere.
> Dig a hole, and the displaced dirt will become a mound elsewhere.

Yes, if you are you digging a hole, then you are also piling a mountain. A higher ground will be created from the carvings of your lowest place; it will become the platform upon which you rise.

Matters of Perspective (One's Whole)

Something grand may appear faint, faded, or diminishing if distanced far from one's grasp.

Something small may become larger, expanded, or unmistakably clear as it finds place closer to one's whole.

These are both matters of perspective.

Someplace in Time

I feel the breeze

I see the clouds drifting
the waters rippling
the sun growing and sinking every day

for these are the movements of our world

And with every movement
I Know
the Earth brings new ground to me

> plates shifting into place
> waters carrying away and bringing toward
> platforms beneath me shaping a path

And may you be upon it

I pray

May this Earth bring you closer
to me every day

until we come to Be
'pon the same plane and claim
how we have surely known
one another before

someplace
    aye, someplace in time

Time (Between)

As I walk forward
my body separates time

> what waits unborn ahead
> from all that has passed behind

This is how we move through space
here on Earthen plane

> always in one place between
> what *will* and what *has* been

Present within a moment
and, again, within the next

> Forwards, backwards, now
> share space
> in every Earthen breath

Time (Forward and Behind)

When you stand to watch me walk away
You keep behind 'thin my time that has been

My whole faces ground that has yet to be claimed
All in my name that will be

And when you turn to walk from me
We both, then, face what is ours to be

Though still behind 'thin other's time
All in one name that has been

Moving forward whilst passed behind
This is our time on the Earth

Pinecones

As discards reunite with source
and move to join our circle's course
they give up self and slowly morph

New life from old

Autumn Leaves

How we ripen and glow
'thin a spectrum of age
and then gently descend for rebirth…

I watch autumn leaves and think about time

    our time
    here on this Earth

Caledonia

High 'pon a stair
of one Cairngorms incline
the bones from one fair
Caledonian
pine rest eternal
supine

limbs and spine weathered bare
though preserved so to serve
and remind rootlings there
'bout the great weights of time
all its Earth-kind must bear
whilst they fare on t'ward the end of Earth-days

On Rainey Park Fields

Out on Rainey Park fields at the East River's edge
I see redbreasts return with the spring
I see Earth break its seals to push out winter's ends
I see traces remain then regrow and transcend

I see movement
I see life
I see sacred assurance that serves to remind

    I, too, shall re-bloom
    and re-gin with new time

Cycle on in rebirth of Earth-days

Traces

My feet leave their marks by the water's glass edge
    one, after two, after three

There in the earth
where all life is bound and cradled
where all life is fed

where all life is warmed and cooled
grown, then claimed

where we bury and, in the end
resurrect

My feet leave their marks by the water's glass edge
    one, after two, after three…after four

Aye, a foot's print will wither
though its bone will endure
and I have wondered the rhyme of this game
oft before

May it be to declare
may it be to remind

> We have Been throughout time
> and one piece from our core
> will remain

Like a Lolling Stone

I am a great Earth-weight. I am
creation of the Great I Am. I am
becoming up from dust in this great Earth-land
and held 'thin the Artist's hand
divine
    melded through the sands and spans of time

I stand, one stone of bedrock frame
    foundation to bind this Earthen plane
wearing slowly and grain by grain by…

slowly as the days of else dance by
A year…a score…ten more dance by
slowly
    and I still remain

I stand alone and tarry in weight. I
tarry and wait a long time. I
keep a tome of current inside
    one power that stirs and never subsides

My force—it pushes and pulls else-tide
Space, I fill
    and I still remain

We—all lolling stones—the same

    rocks of age unknown—the veins
    and bones 'neath land and sea foam graves

Each silent, patient, ancient sage
who has Been and Seen since Birth, it seems
will remain 'til the end of Earth-days

Peace

Peace is something I have yet to know

past two powder-soft palmfuls of rich chocolate earth
gently gleaned from the grounds of Allean's forest-church
'midst her stillness of wisdom and silence of verse
'midst her clean morning fragrance of life and rebirth
Past one temple of trees where my soul-spirit grows

peace is something I have yet to know

Of the Sea

The Ocean

Where every ripple
vibrates
with the tranquility of a Chopin nocturne

Where every wave
crashes
with the passion of a Bizet symphony

Notes on the Sea

Looking up from down upon the Earth, it is easy to gauge the vast span of the sky.

Looking down, it is impossible to view the depth beneath the soil, though it is an expanse just the same.

These realms remain unknown to us, for they are places where humankind may not Be. The surface land is where we have been crafted to dwell, though it, too, comes with exceptions: the hottest deserts, the polar deserts, the rockiest mountains, and the highest volcanic peaks. Our traces are scarce upon Earth's most remote islands, and they are swallowed within its seas.

> No, this sphere is not mine nor any other egocentric human's—no, not any of these Earthen lands and most certainly not its seas.

The water—it connects all things on Earth. It exists in all creation, and it comprises every element of our own physical form. It cures. It nourishes. It refreshes. It renews. It is the beginning, and it is the end, for all life began in the sea, and all life can be reclaimed by its swift and surging force.

> No, this sphere is not mine nor any other egocentric human's—no, not any of these Earthen lands and most certainly not its seas.

One Whole

I notice that water holds no shape of its own
and never strives to stand 'lone
but to serve

an ocean
a sea
a river
a stream
as always
one part of one whole

A wave meets the shore, and its waters displace
reaching wide 'cross the sand
as though searching for space

    seeping down into earth
    dissipating in air
    ebbing back to the shares
    of one whole

This is movement

This is life

To give up one's self is one
great sacrifice

    taking form, changing phase
    at the Earth's will and grace
    as always
    one part of one whole

Pas de deux

As I bathe
supine
my form in prime
is one mountainous terrain
that has swollen through time

Water

sits with each stillness
or stirs with each breath
for a Humphrey and Weidmanesque
pas de deux-et

Water
flows to claim space
where my high peaks submerge
then recedes
from the place
where they rise

Falling
Recovering
Moving in
Moving out

On this Earth
we are motion and shift

Making Waves

Ideas

>are as boats
>gracefully
>gliding across the sea
>
>disrupting surrounding idleness
>and creating new movement with tidal shifts
>from wherever their hulls may be
>
>These waves becalm
>These swells become subtle
>never quelled
>for the waters cannot hold one place
>
>undulating
>outwards
>further
>and still
>
>crashing and clashing
>with what comes 'cross their way
>
>pulling back from the shores
>'sorbing into the mass
>serving
>as part of one whole

Movement

Movement forged 'thin the waters
may be eyed 'cross full 'spanse
though the greatest displays
are crashes as waves
clash against all proud and fixed
'thin one way

Movement is power
    she changes her world
Drops of seawater spray
    sweat and tears. Her exertions
stay behind as reminders

Each salient assertion
of what had once been
and what now should be

carries forth with the birth
of Earth-days

From You to Me

I gaze upon the water
Skim my hand atop its glass

I wonder if the same drops
Have ever held your wooden ketch in path

Upon the sea then found their way
Across the Earthen Down's blue 'spanse

That keeps 'tween you and me, my love
Keeps vast 'tween you and me

The waters—they are moving: always sending out
Or bringing t'ward

Or melding force with one another
Joining Earth along its courses

For these are their ways
And how I pray

There may be one so carefully laid
To flow across the Down

From you to me with love
May it carry you across the Earthen Down

To me for love

Explorers of a Boundless Deep

Diving

far into corners
of a dark place

    down

far down
to uncover unknown

    Aye
    those who are born
    to swim down through thought
    are explorers of a boundless deep

Submergence

Shallow water

> I tread there
> lightly
> and sense with one toe
> or one wary hand

How quickly vibrations surcease
How clearly
every small thing beneath
can be seen

I bring a courteous smile
for the simple and mundane
for the empty shells and wave-battered
bones of what's been

for the trash that erodes
preserves, or remains

Thoughtless discoveries are surface-level-known

But the deep

> my gaze grasps
> its opaque, gray glass
> and I plunge as far down
> as my life-breath will last

There is pressure
and darkness
There are forms of great mass
kept unseen in the arms of a shadow

The vast

    you must look there with wide eyes
    and See there with wise eyes

A thoughtful discovery
is to wonder and find
what has never been found
what has never been known
Oh explorer, hold fast to all
Earthen unbound!

Always go farther
then farther
and still

    Submergence deep into the Down

To Source

Flow East, north—retrace
your way upstream to source

Hell Gate's waters keep the course
to follow Home
    aye, follow Home

I Go to the Water

Water will keep us in constant motion—it lives in shift: It keeps afloat, it carries along, it crashes and drowns, it erodes, and it gently washes away.

And so, I go to the water for change. I am pulled there often when things seem dark or when things become unbalanced. I speak in silence with the Great Artist who molds its fine liquid media, and I wait in hope for my past traces to be washed away.

There at the water's rippling glass edge, my soul—my whole—is cleansed, and I leave thankful to have known such a peace.

At the Edges of Seas

At the edges of seas
On the sands of their shores

Where the soles of men's feet
Meet the gates of world lore

And the souls of men bleat
To find rest 'pon salt graves

With a sadness to mourn
Past the 'spanse of all gaze

Many will stand 'fore an ocean or sea
Much will be cast to be drowned

Or carried adrift 'yond the cities of men
And then gathered once 'gain by the Crowned

Transform

I have seen the waters carry away
I have watched them bring forth to the shore

I wait here
upon these sands of dry earth
to cast out

to receive
and transform

Beauty in the Broken (Sea Glass)

Emptied and discarded shells shatter to sharp shards, scatter to the sands from which they first came, and then begin their transformations within sacred and salty seas.

>With time, roughened edges heal.
>With time, fragility strengthens.

In time, troves of tinkling treasures trickle to shore—to be gathered within the loving hands of those who find beauty in what is broken.

Reflections

I have seen many stand at the East River's edge
gazing silently down 'nto its looking glass
and I have wondered

> *What is carried as heft in each heart?*
> *Is it wished to be washed clean away?*

Our reflections in water are rippled and hazed
Might it be that our selves have enough room for change?
Might it be that our selves are not clearly defined?

Life is movement
Life is motion and shift. Aye

if the waters could capture with liquescent lens
every moment of redemption
'fore a baptismal cleanse…

These stills in collection

> *Reflections in the Earth's Mirrored Pools*

> A Thoreau tribute—airy
> unpenned moody-blues…
> Friedrichesque allegories…

Oh, the stories we'd know
'bout our time on this plane—how we've shed human self
then en-lightened
inclined to up-rise

The Holy Sea

The water fills
The water rids
Its 'spanse
    one wholly see
It Is a blessed brine
baptismal shrine
    one sacred, holy sea

Washed Away

At one time during late summer, I walked along the Hallet's Cove sandy beach, leaving my trail of footsteps behind.

Days later, I reapproached the same beach only to find that the East River's waters had swelled to swallow its shore.

This bittersweet moment left me torn—between feelings of sadness for all those moments that will become but a memory

and feelings of relief for the assurance that past traces can, ultimately, be washed away.

Trinity

Along the Hudson—white and whist
lolls Feb'rary at laze amidst
each steady tone of engine drone
and icy, northbound steel rail kiss

Behind one frosted pane transfixed

> an offish New York finance prince
> who keeps his views skewed down in "news"
> and black-inked, boldface politics

Though poets' eyes gaze left then lift
'yond out to where the water sits
beneath each row of bricked ice tow
and lofty resurrection mist

Trinity transforms to how the Earth need be

Purest state, embodiment, and trace exposed
as farther sun warms holy coast

Forge

Whenever you must Go
like a river, flow there—flow

Let your power carve each obstacle
and forge a way t'ward Whole

The Up and the Sea

Far wide in expanse
Far deep in blue scheme

A reflection, the Up and the sea

Momentum

A gull dives
down, plunging fast

    down to skim past
    the ocean and
    its mirrored glass

Is it pride from a catch
or disappointment from an empty grasp?

Is it only velocity
or also, perhaps
an awakening

from that one
brief
glance of reflection
and a splash of baptismal brine?

Perhaps…

Perhaps they are all
momentum
to pull up on our paths
and soar

Peace (Reprise)

Peace is something I have yet to know

past two powder-soft palmfuls of rich chocolate earth
gently gleaned from the grounds of Allean's forest-church
'midst her stillness of wisdom and silence of verse
'midst her clean morning fragrance of life and rebirth
Past one temple of trees where my soul spirit grows

peace is something I have yet to know

Past the come-hither scents from the North's salted brine
past its toe-tickling sprays of baptismal sublime
past the sherbet sky's dreams 'loft a sinking sun's gleams
'bed sea ripples that trickle in free-water time
past my mere-ness that meres whilst blue 'spanse ever grows

peace is something I have yet to know

Epilogue: Here on This Earth

Whenever I muster the gall to stand alongside the power of our incredible Earth, I can only help but feel more human. As tiny and as insignificant as I wish this humanness to be, it stays so heavily weighted within me. It is humbling: I feel my place as I surrender to something much greater than I could ever know of myself. The sounds and sights of all that I see every day—all that I have seemingly come to recognize like the back of my hand—suddenly become more charged, more powerful, and more alive. I carefully watch how the natural world operates—how slow and simple it can all seem to be. Connections are made: I understand why some things happen as they do and how they might relate to a similar happening within my own life. Sometimes, however, there are no epiphanies. Sometimes there are just moments of peace, fulfillment, and contentment with nonanswers—moments that simply allow for wonderment, the formulation of additional questions, and the developing awareness of a rather vast canvas of existence and design that is so infinitely greater than our very own being.

What is our place?

I ponder this every time I descend from Earth's terrestrial doorstep, noting the weight of each weary and rooted foot as it carries me to my human home.

It is as you are now; it is bound down to this Earth.

What, then, CAN be our place?

Aye, we are of a curious human nature.
I have wandered, noticed, and wondered myself quite often into Knowing, and I Know now that there is, indeed, a balance to everything.

It is not as you are now; it is unbound to this Earth.

And so, I turn my thoughts toward all I know that is not of this downward plane, and I look up—high above the Earth.

Glossary (Who?)

GOD, HE, YOUR, GRAVITY, SOMETHING, SPIRIT, I AM, ARTIST, HOME, CROWNED, TRINITY, WHOLE, POWER, LOVE, HIGHEST, HIS
A high power is a great power, indeed, though a higher power is much greater. The highest power is both the Greatest Power and Greatest Love known, for the Highest has given form to all things that Are and will allow for all forms to Be. With what name have you called your Highest?

I
I am. I am mere—aye, so very mere, indeed.

(DORIS) HUMPHREY AND (CHARLES) WEIDMAN
There is a *pas de deux* in all that we do: a negative space to hug each positive space and a recovery to respond to each fall.

(HENRY DAVID) THOREAU
"I must stay alone and know that I am alone to contemplate and feel nature in full; I have to surrender myself to what encircles me, I have to merge with my clouds and rocks in order to be what I am."
~Caspar David Friedrich

Scholle, Andreas. (2000). Authenticity and Fiction in the Russian Literary Journey, 1790-1840. In Russian Research Center Studies (Vol. 92, p. 108). Cambridge, Mass: Harvard University Press.

(CASPAR DAVID) FRIEDRICH
"Could a greater miracle take place than for us to look through each other's eyes for an instant?"
~Henry David Thoreau

Thoreau, Henry D. Walden, Or, Life in the Woods. London: J.M. Dent, 1908.

(Georges) Bizet
Have you heard an ocean's wave crash? If so, then you have surely heard the cymbals in *Carmen*.

(Frederic) Chopin
I see "Waltz No. 7 in C-Sharp Minor, Op. 64 No. 2" as the color yellow not because I have chromesthesia but because I have grapheme-color synesthesia, and my color for the number seven is yellow. I have heard "Waltz No. 7 in C-Sharp Minor, Op. 64 No. 2" with my two feet bare and pressing down into a familiar Marley floor.

Glossary (Where?)

DOWN, EARTH
You are here, and I am here as well, for here we are bound to live amongst all Earth-kind for all our Earth-days. How many Earth-kind have you known? How many Earth-kind have you loved?

UP
You are not there, nor am I, for the Up is a place high above the Earth, and to reach it, we must Rise.

SMALL
Often, you must bend very far forward or down very low to find Earth's wee-places, though the Small are vast and filled with Great wee-wisdom. Have you ever spied inside a pinecone? Have you ever seen between the petals of a wildflower?

(THE) TROSSACHS, (LOCH) ARD, CAIRNGORMS (NATIONAL PARK), CALEDONIA, ALLEAN (FOREST), NORTH (SEA)
In Scotland, you can feel the passage of time with your feet pressed down upon its earth. This, I do swear, for a self of mine remains behind someplace in Scotland—behind someplace in its time.

NEW YORK (CITY)
Here you may live amongst countless Earth-kind intimately, though to live as such, you must know a peace with them all. Where have you found your peace?

HUDSON (RIVER)
I retrace this path often from the harbor t'ward source, and I remember all that has passed 'thin my time.

Astoria, Hell Gate, East / East River, Hallet's Cove, Rainey / Rainey Park

There is portokalopita in Astoria—everywhere in Astoria—and there is yemista and spanakopita and tirokafteri and saganaki, and there are kourabiedes almost as perfect as the ones my yia-yia once made. This is why it feels so much like home—aye, so very much like Cypress Hills in 1989.

At Hell Gate, you can see a turbulent East River swirling, waving, crashing, and swaying with one part of its plane flowing south toward New York Harbor and another running parallel but north toward its source. There is a beautiful choreography about it all, and Shore Boulevard is prime seating for such performances: the coveted front row in Hell Gate Theatre's raised mezzanine. And when you look down from there—down directly to where the stage edges upon East's Astorian banks—you will see the theatre's treasured orchestra and its world-famous sea glass section. Hear them chime divine hymns like a Sunday morning church handbell choir as each beached wave lurches forward or retreats to Whole. Hear the deep, resounding bellows of the Triboro overhead, and witness the unmatched acoustics with which its understructure creates. Note: There is no curtain call upon this stage. There is no bow nor pause for glory by performer nor maestro. No, there is no ego brought forth by this Earth.

In Long Island City, you will find flocks of animated seagulls gathering at Hallet's Cove as though assuming roles within a Richard Bach allegory. You might also see cormorants traveling downriver from Astoria and doing all those things cormorants must do. Sometimes I play a game with the cormorants: I note where in the river they plunge and then guess where in the river they will re-emerge. We play, and we both amuse, for my guesses are laughable at best, and the cormorants are much wiser than I: I am mere—aye, so very mere, indeed.

There are mated pairs of mockingbirds and red-tailed hawks at Rainey Park. There are red-breasted robins flooding Rainey's clover fields in spring and graffiti messages that pop up synchronously whenever one, such as I, is looking for meaning. In Rainey Park, I have never felt alone, for there is a peace here in Long Island City, and for that, I am humbly grateful.

Glossary (Why?)

GREATER, ARE, BEING, LOVE, BE, BECOME, GREAT, GROW, GO, KNOW, BEEN, SEEN, BIRTH, SEE, IS, KNOWING, GREATEST, ART, RISE

Aye, we are here on this Earth, though sometimes I have written that we Are. And just as I have written about all that my own eyes have seen across Earth-land, I have also noted what my self has Seen. This has always been the case after experiencing the Highest within His Art, for I believe that in those moments, divinity has filled my eyes and transcended my sight into a higher vision. Similarly, and at other times, love has become a higher love, presence has become a higher presence, and thought has become a higher thought—as they have and always will for those who connect with the Earth.

What's Next:
Up
High Above the Earth

Elsewhere

Here on this Earth
I roam, and I search
outwards
upwards
then higher still
but always elsewhere

for we are born
knowing
there is someplace else

and to reach it
we must Rise

Copyright © 2021 by Sparrow Santo.
Published by Little Bird Press.
ISBN: 978-0-578775-77-7

Cover photo by Sparrow Santo.
Cover photo editing and author photo by Joe DeAngelis.

All rights reserved. Printed in the United States of America. No part of this book may be used or reproduced in any manner whatsoever without written permission except in the case of brief quotations embodied in critical articles and reviews.

First edition. Library of Congress Cataloging in Publication Data is available.

www.ingramcontent.com/pod-product-compliance
Lightning Source LLC
Chambersburg PA
CBHW072019290426
44109CB00018B/2286